Andrew Bianchi & Andy Gray

Scripture Union, 207–209 Queensway, Bletchley, Milton Keynes, MK2 2EB, England.
Email: info@scriptureunion.org.uk
Website: www.scriptureunion.org.uk

Scripture Union Australia
Locked Bag 2, Central Coast Business Centre, NSW 2252
Website: www.scriptureunion.org.au

Scripture Union USA
PO Box 987, Valley Forge, PA 19482
Website: www.scriptureunion.org

British Library Cataloguing-in-Publication Data.
A catalogue record of this book is available from the British Library.

Printed and bound in Malta by Interprint.

Cover design: fourninezero design

& Scripture Union is an international Christian charity working with churches in more than 130 countries, providing resources to bring the good news about Jesus Christ to children, young people and families and to encourage them to develop spiritually through the Bible and prayer.

As well as our network of volunteers, staff and associates who run holidays, church-based events and school Christian groups, we produce a wide range of publications and support those who use our resources through training programmes.

This book belongs to:

....

son/daughter of

....

son/daughter of

....

of the tribe of

....

Turn to page 32 to find out how to fill in your certificate!

CONTENTS

THE BEGINNING BIT:
GOD'S RULES

The ten commandments are old. Very old. They first appeared thousands of years ago. This makes them even older than your school rules and (probably) older than most of your teachers. You can read about them (the commandments, not your teachers) in the second book of the Bible, called Exodus. Or you can read the next few sentences.

God sent a man called Moses to rescue a people called the Israelites from a life of slavery. On the way to their new land, they stopped at a mountain called Sinai. Moses went up the mountain and there God spoke to him, giving him ten special rules that would help the Israelites to live happily together in their new home. But perhaps more importantly, these rules would always remind them that God was really important.

The rest of the Bible is about how good the Israelites were at obeying these ten rules. It tells stories about what happened when they got it right (which didn't happen very often). And more stories about when they got it wrong (which is most of the time). There is even one person who got full marks.

One thing is clear. Life was far better for the people when they did exactly what God said, as I think you'll agree…

PUT ME FIRST.
DON'T HAVE ANY OTHER GODS

There is one simple reason why God wants his people not to have any other gods. He is the only real God in the universe. If anybody else claims to have another god, they're wrong. Sometimes the Bible talks about other gods, but as far as God is concerned, they aren't gods at all. God is God and that's that.

God's the man!

When God saved his people from slavery in Egypt, it wasn't just a simple rescue mission. He also had a point to prove. The point was this. He is the most powerful being in the whole universe!

You see, Pharaoh couldn't stop God. The Egyptians couldn't stop him, and the things they thought were gods certainly couldn't stop him. Pharaoh was a bit stubborn and it took him a long time to realise this. When Moses asked to take the people of Israel out of Egypt, Pharaoh refused. So God sent a series of bad events, called plagues, to make him change his mind. He did... eventually... but not before some pretty dreadful things had happened.

Just before the last plague, God told Moses that he was going to bring a final judgement upon the gods of Egypt. He was going to show them up for what they really were. Nothing. This last plague was the worst of the lot. It killed every firstborn child in every Egyptian family in every corner of Egypt. Sadly, it was only at this point that Pharaoh realised that God was the tops.

I hope you get itchy

God told his people that lots of bad things would happen to them if they forgot about him and chased after other gods. Moses wrote them down in the form of sayings, called curses. A curse is a promise that something horrible is going to happen. Can you guess which are the real threats and which are made up ones?

1)   *They would be cursed in the country.*

2)   *They would be cursed in the city.*

       (In other words, everywhere.)

3)   *They would have dreadful baskets.*

4)   *They would make rotten bread.*

5)   *Their children would be cursed.*

6) *They would grow useless crops.*

7) *All their animals would suffer.*

8) *They would be confused.*

9) *They would suffer from a wasting disease.*

10) *They would get fevers.*

11) *They would suffer from inflammation
(whatever that is).*

12) *It would be too hot.*

13) *There wouldn't be enough water.*

14) *They would get mildew in their homes.*

15) *There would be no rain.*

16) *The ground would become dry and hard.*

17) *They would lose all their battles.*

18) *Their bodies would be eaten by birds and animals.*

19) *They would suffer from boils.*

20) *They would itch.*

21) *They would get tumours.*

22) *They would suffer from sores.*

23) *They would go mad.*

24) *They would go blind.*

25) *They would be confused.*

26) They would be robbed.

27) Men would be ready to get married then someone else would take their bride away.

28) They would build a house and then not live in it.

29) They would plant a vineyard and not enjoy any of its wine.

30) Their cattle would be killed but they wouldn't eat any of the meat.

31) Their donkeys would be stolen (along with sheep and other animals).

32) They would be slaves like they were in Egypt.

33) They would be taken away to another country.

34) Locusts would eat all the crops.

35) They would live in constant fear of everything.

Believe it or not, all of these were real curses said against the Israelites. In other words, if they worshipped other gods, everything would get as bad as it possibly could. They seem a bit over the top to us, but they show how serious God was about his people sticking with him.

On the plus side, there were also lots of nice promises if the people just worshipped the one true God. Not only would they not suffer any of these things, but they would have a great time. Everything they did would be a success and they would live happily in the land, forever.

Get lost!

Matthew 4

Just before Jesus started doing miracles and teaching about God, he went away on his own to a wild, desert place. While he was there he was tempted to disobey God. Satan told him to bow down at his feet and worship him. He promised that he would make Jesus ruler of the world. But Jesus wasn't having any of it. He told Satan to get lost. He quoted a part of the Bible which said that people were only to worship God and to do what he wanted. Satan knew that he wasn't going to catch Jesus out and so he did as he was told and went away.

Make your mind up!

Acts 14

On one occasion, the apostle* Paul was telling people about Jesus at a place called Lystra. There was a lame man in the crowd. Paul turned to him and told him to get up. Immediately he bounced onto his legs and started walking around.

As you can imagine the crowd went wild with excitement. They thought this was fantastic. They shouted out, "The gods have come to earth!" at the top of their voices. They gave Paul the name Hermes, and his friend Barnabas they called Zeus. Then the priest who looked after the nearby temple of Zeus fetched some bulls and flowers in order to make a sacrifice to the two of them.

GODS? I **THOUGHT** ONE OF THEM HAD LOST A CONTACT LENS!!

An apostle means someone who was one of the first Christian teachers. Apostles told people about Jesus.

Paul and Barnabas didn't like the idea of that at all. They tore their clothes (this was their way of showing how upset they were) and told everyone to stop. "We are just like you – human beings. All we're doing is telling you not to follow useless gods, but to worship the one God who made everything. He is the one who has given you all the good things that you enjoy."

Paul is bad for business
Acts 19

In New Testament times there was a lot of money to be made out of the god industry. One man called Demetrius used to make silver shrines for a god in Ephesus, called Artemis. He was getting fed up with Paul, because he was ruining his business! So he called together some of his mates saying, "That Paul claims that the gods we make aren't gods at all. If he carries on like this not only will our wonderful business get a bad name, but people will think badly of Artemis and her temple. We've got to do something!"

His words got them going and they all started shouting, "Long live Artemis of the Ephesians!" (An Ephesian is someone who lives in Ephesus.) Pretty soon the whole city went berserk and some of Paul's friends were seized by the mob. They took them to one of the important men in the city. The words "Long live Artemis of the Ephesians!" echoed through the air for two whole hours.

Finally, the top man managed to calm everybody down. He was worried because if the Romans heard about the riot they would blame him. In the end he sent everybody home and Paul left to go elsewhere.

A gathering of gods

Despite all the warnings, the Israelites often followed other gods. Sometimes it would be just one god. Sometimes it would be several gods. At one time in their history they followed seven different gods — one for every day of the week. They were the gods of Baal, the gods called Ashtoreths, the gods of Aram, the gods of Sidon, the gods of Moab, the gods of the Ammonites and the gods of the Philistines.

IF IT'S WEDNESDAY, IT MUST BE MOAB

My God's so cool, he's hot!
I Kings 18

Elijah the prophet was not pleased that the Israelites were following the god Baal. So he set up a big fight.

As you can imagine, everybody wanted to be at the big fight. There was a roar of appreciation as the 450 prophets of Baal stepped into the ring. Then as Elijah jumped over the ropes there were boos and heckling from the onlookers.

"Ladies and gentlemen, this is a contest between two gods. In the right hand corner we have Baal, current Israelite champion and defending trans-Caanan gold medallist.

"And in the left corner we have... God, creator of the whole world and saviour of the people of Israel on numerous occasions. He's fallen out of favour recently, but today could be his big comeback!

"Fighting for Baal we have 450 of his best praying prophets. And for God – just Elijah. He'll need to be on his toes to get through this one!

"Today is decision time. You Israelites must follow either God or Baal. The winner is the one whose god can set these bulls alight. No matches. No illegal use of Bunsen burners or welding torches. You just have to pray to your god, asking him to light the fire. Only the true God will be able to do it."

And with that, the prophets of Baal step up onto the field of play. They choose one of the bulls and away they go. After a short while, the bull is ready to be burnt up. The only trouble

ER... CAN I **JUST** HAVE A WORD?

is, nothing happens. From early morning until midday they scream and shout and rant and rave, but not even a spark or a flicker comes from heaven.

This really annoyed the prophets, so they shouted louder and louder and began cutting themselves in their frenzy. But still nothing happened. Several hours later, in the evening, the bull was still there, not even cooked.

Then Elijah stepped up. He dug a large ditch around the altar. He cut the bull up according to the best recipe in the book and then he poured water over it. Not once. Not twice, but three times. The water squelched down into the trench. Then at just the right time, he stepped up. All the eyes of the crowd were on him.

And with that a huge ball of fire came down from heaven and burned up the bull. Even the water in the ditch evaporated away. The crowd went wild with excitement. "The Lord is God. The Lord is God!" they chanted, and at Elijah's command they grabbed hold of the prophets of Baal and executed them.

Elijah had shown that there really was only one God, and to try and pretend otherwise was just a waste of time.

"Put me first. Don't have any other gods." God told his people to do this because he is the only real God in the universe! He'd also helped his people in so many ways. When we think of all the good things in life and realise God is behind them all, it seems only fair to make him the number one influence in everything we do!

DON'T MAKE ANY OBJECT AND THEN BOW DOWN AND WORSHIP IT AS THOUGH IT WERE A GOD.

I AM THE ONLY ONE WHO DESERVES TO BE WORSHIPPED.

Did you know that this is one of the first broken rules we can read about in the Bible?

You want a god?
Exodus 32

The trouble was that when Moses went up onto the mountain to talk to God, the people left down on the ground got a bit impatient. They began complaining to Aaron, Moses' brother.

And then
someone said:

"Yes, after all, it's not like we've got
any rules about stuff like that, is it?"

By this stage, Aaron was probably a bit fed up with his brother, too. Going off like that and leaving him in charge. As if he knew anything about desert living! So he came up with a plan.

When Aaron recovered after his shock, he took the earrings back to his tent and all kinds of crashing and banging could be heard...When he'd finished, he called all the people together again.

"Da da! People without earrings! Children of Israel! It gives me great pleasure to present to you, on this day... your new god."

Then Aaron continued: "If you all come back tomorrow we will have a party and enjoy singing, dancing, drinking and eating. Come and look your best. Put on your finest jewellery, your best earr... oops, sorry. Well, just come tomorrow."
And they did.
So, there we have it. God's rule was broken!

Now, God knew what the people were doing and he sent Moses back down the mountain. Moses wasn't a happy man when he saw what was going on. He smashed the tablets of stone with the 10 rules on them and gave Aaron a right telling off. Moses was so angry that he ordered the priests to kill those who had turned their backs on God in this way. That day 3,000 Israelites died. And all because of the golden calf that they pretended was their new god.

Aaron got off pretty lightly. Which is more than can be said for the calf. Moses took it and threw it into a fire. Then he smashed it up until it was like a fine powder. Not content with that, he mixed it with water and... believe it or not, he made the Israelites drink the water!

Two calves don't make a whole lot of sense
1 Kings 12

You'd have thought that Israel's history teachers would have warned everyone about idols and calves, but if they did, at least one person didn't learn the lesson. Many years after Moses and Aaron's time, there was a king called Jeroboam. He decided to make not one, but TWO golden calves, and put them in places called Dan and Bethel. What's more, like Aaron before him, he told the people that these cows were the gods that had brought them out of Egypt. (It didn't seem to matter to him that the calves hadn't even been made when the Israelites escaped from Egypt – but I did say he probably wasn't very good at history.)

God sent a prophet to tell Jeroboam off. Jeroboam ordered his men to grab the prophet, but as soon as Jeroboam pointed his finger at the prophet, Jeroboam's hand became old and wrinkled. (It is rude to point after all.) This freaked Jeroboam out and he asked the prophet to pray for him. When he prayed, the hand got better. But did the king learn? Not a bit. He spent the rest of his life doing the wrong thing and brought a lot of trouble on his people.

Names of idols

Baal: Baal was the main god
of the people who lived in the land that God gave the Israelites. He was often thought to be a god of storms.

LOOKS LIKE THERE'S A BAAL BREWING

Asherah: Asherah was a goddess of the sea. The Bible talks a lot about things called Asherah poles, which were probably made of wood. God was forever telling his people to cut down Asherah poles.

JUST OFF TO DO A BIT OF *ASHERAH* CHOPPING DEAR ...

Teraphim: These may have been idols that some people kept in their homes. They would have been small and easy to carry.

One good thing to do with an old idol
2 Kings 10

One of the better kings of Israel (and there weren't that many) was called Jehu. He destroyed some of the idols of Baal and ripped up the temple where they had been standing.

But the best bit is to come! What do you think he did with the ruins?

(a)   **Opened up a museum.**
(b)   **Sold the stones to a local builders merchant.**
(c)   **Used it as a toilet.**
(d)   **Built a temple to God.**

The answer is (c). He turned it into a public toilet – which is one way of showing what you think of an idol.

Really stupid!
Isaiah 44

One of the funniest bits of the Bible is where God shows how stupid it is for anybody to make an idol and then bow down to it. You can try this at home if you have a spare tree that your parents don't mind you chopping down. All you need is an axe or electric saw, strong muscles and a few matches.

1) First chop the tree down.
2) Then cut it into two parts.
3) Choose one part (eeny meeny miney mo etc).
4) Make that part into a nice idol sort of shape.
5) Build a fire using the other bit.
6) Keep warm and worship the idol.
7) Think hard about what you have just done.

What you have just done is really stupid. Why? One bit of the tree you turned into an idol, and the other bit you turned into a fire so you could sit down, keep warm and be idle. It just doesn't make sense, deciding one bit is a god and the other bit is only good for throwing on the fire. God says that anyone who thinks they've made a god in this way is just being plain stupid.

Did you know that the Philistines (long-time enemies of God s people) used to carry their idols into battle as good luck charms?

ΥΥΥΥΥΥΥΥΥΥΥΥΥΥΥΥΥΥ

Many years later, Jesus follower, Paul, was really upset. Everywhere he went in Athens, Greece, there were idols. He even found a statue with a note saying it was put there in honour of a god no one knew! So he took this as a good opportunity to tell people about the real God.

Gideon – Idol Smasher
Judges 6

Gideon battled Midian
With some men who drank like dogs
But before he was a soldier
He turned idols into logs!

After they came into the special land that God had given them, there was a long period of time when the Israelites forgot about him. When this happened their enemies made them suffer. Every now and then God would pick someone to help the Israelites. One such person was called Gideon.

He was busy one day when an angel told him to defeat the latest enemies called the Midianites. Before he could do that he was told he had to pull down some of his father's idols. So, in the middle of the night he got ten of his servants and they took down the idols. Gideon then built an altar to God. He used the wood from one of the idols to make a fire.

When the people of the town discovered what had happened, they got really angry with Gideon and wanted to kill him. His father, Joash, stepped in.

"If Baal really is a god, then he can look after himself when someone tries to damage his altar. Let him sort it out."
And of course, he never did. Because he couldn't. Because he wasn't God!

I don't suppose you've ever sat down and made an idol. But you may have tried to imagine what God is like or how you'd like him to be. The Bible says we don't need to do that because God has shown us what he is like. If we want to know what God is like… how he thinks… what he does… we only have to read the stories about Jesus. Because Jesus is God. So remember – don't idle away your time making idols, because Jesus is ideal.

DON'T SAY BAD THINGS ABOUT GOD
OR USE HIS NAME AS IF IT WERE A BAD WORD

Have you ever been called a froward fat-kidneyed horn-beast? Or possibly a currish weather-bitten canker-blossom? No, neither have I, but if we'd lived several hundred years ago we might have been. Or even worse, we might have used them on somebody else.

No one likes to be called names. But imagine how you would feel if every time someone was cross or angry they said your name.

That is probably how God feels every time someone says his name when they are surprised or feeling fed up. Or what about if you found out that people were making fun of you all the time?

In the Bible, when it is God on the receiving end of those sorts of things, it is called blasphemy. And it's a very serious thing to do as this story shows.

What did you just say?
Leviticus 24

When the Israelites left Egypt, not only did they bring out their furniture, animals and clothes – a few of them brought some Egyptians with them. One such woman had married an Egyptian. Her name was Shelomith. Her dad's name was Dibri. He belonged to the tribe of Israelites called the Danites. (You may be wondering why I've told you this. Well, people in the Bible liked to know who their parents and grandparents were, as well as which group they belonged to. If I'd been around then they would have called me Andrew, son of Eric, son of Frederick, of the tribe of Bianchi. If you look on page 3 of this book, you'll see that you can put your name in this way.) Anyway, back to Shelomith and her husband. They had a son. We don't know his name so we'll call him Egyptoid. Not a popular name, I know, but then as you'll see by the end of the story, he wasn't a popular lad.

As often happens in the Bible, Egyptoid got into a fight with someone whose parents were both Israelites. During the fight, as well as hitting, punching, kicking, scratching, hair pulling and biting, he blasphemed against God's name. We don't know what he said exactly but whatever it was, other people heard it and they knew it wasn't very nice.

The people who had been watching the fight dashed off to Moses, the leader, to see what they should do. He wasn't sure, so he told them to put Egyptoid into prison while they waited to see what God himself thought of his name being badly used.

What God told them was very bad news for Egyptoid. First of all they had to take him out of the camp. Then all those who had heard him say the bad thing were to put their hands on him. And then – and this is the gruesome bit – everybody had to pick up a stone and throw it at him until Egyptoid died. God then said that this was to happen every time someone blasphemed. It didn't matter whether the person was an Israelite or a foreigner or half-Israelite, the punishment was always to be the same.

As well as saying bad things about God, it was also possible to blaspheme by saying bad things about people who God had chosen to do something special for him. This can be summed up in a verse found in the book of Numbers which says, "Don't blaspheme God or curse the ruler of your people."

The point was that God had put the king in charge of the country. So to say nasty things against the king was a bit like thinking it was a bad idea of God's to make that person important.

Don't lie to me about blasphemy
(try saying that ten times in a hurry!)
1 Kings 21

A man called Naboth owned a vineyard. The trouble was that the king, Ahab, wanted to have it too. When Naboth wouldn't sell it to him, Ahab's wife, Jezebel, got some bad people to say untrue things about Naboth. These wicked men accused Naboth of having said bad things about God and the king. It was a pack of lies, of course, but Jezebel knew Naboth would get into a lot of trouble if people believed he had said those things. It did. They killed him (see the chapter about longing to have something that belongs to someone else for the details of this dreadful deed).

King Curse

2 Samuel 16

David had lots of sons — at least twenty of them. It could be something to do with the fact that he had at least nine wives and probably a lot more. David s sons had fantastic names like Eliphelet, Kileab and Shobab.

There is a strange story about a man who cursed King David. It all began when Absalom, one of David's sons, led a rebellion to try and become king in his place.

David managed to escape with some of his loyal followers. A man called Shimei saw them running away and began throwing stones at the king. He also started to blaspheme and curse the king.

David's friends wanted to go and sort him out. But David told them not to bother. He wasn't planning to kill his own son Absalom for plotting against him, so he certainly wasn't going to kill anyone else for saying nasty things.

Most people who tried to defeat David, ended up losing (just ask Goliath). Absalom was no exception. His army was defeated by David's commanders and he was killed when his hair got caught in the branches of an oak tree. David's position as king was safe and lots of people came to him to apologise for having tried to get rid of him.

Shimei was one of those who came to say sorry. One of David's friends, Abishai, wanted to kill Shimei, but the king wasn't interested.

And he promised Shimei that he wouldn't kill him. Which is more or less what happened. I say more or less because... no. You wouldn't want to know. After all it's a bit nasty and devious and I know that sort of stuff doesn't interest you...

Oh, all right then. But don't say I didn't warn you. And don't go thinking that David was a squeaky-clean sort of person. He wasn't.

You see, David didn't want to kill Shimei there and then, but he did want him to die. And because he was the king I suppose he thought he could wait a bit. In fact he waited until he was just about ready to die himself....

When David was a lot older, he told his son Solomon to come and see him. And this is what he said.

"Solomon, my dear son. Do you remember Shimei, son of Gera?"

"The one who said all those things about you?"

"Yes," replied his father as he smashed a goblet down in anger. "That's the one."

"Yes, I remember him."

"Well in a moment of kindness I promised him I wouldn't kill him for all those cruel words. And I'm going to stick by them. But I was wondering. Could you do me a favour?"

"OK."

"It's just, well. I'd quite like it if you could cover his grey hairs with a bit of colour. Sort of blood colour."

"What? Some highlights?"

"No! Don't be so stupid!"

"Are you calling me stupid? I would have thought that's the last thing anyone could call me."*

"I don't want him to die a natural death. The red stuff has got to be his own blood."

"You mean you want me to kill him?"

"At last. You're going to have to be a bit brighter than that if you want to be king, my son."

Then David died. Although he had promised he wasn't going to kill Shimei himself, he was going to make sure he was going to die for what he had done. Perhaps as he got older, David regretted having made the promise, but rather than break it, he got Solomon to do his dirty business. So that was the end of Shimei.

God told me...
2 Kings 18

For a book that's supposed to be about love, there is a lot of fighting in the Bible. Everyone seems to do it — but especially the kings. They couldn't be happier than when invading another country, besieging a city or stabbing and poking a few enemies here and there. What makes it worse is that they had such dreadful names. Take this story for example...

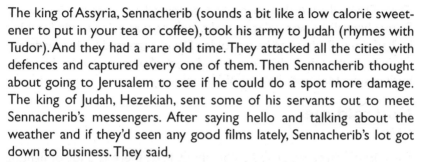

The king of Assyria, Sennacherib (sounds a bit like a low calorie sweetener to put in your tea or coffee), took his army to Judah (rhymes with Tudor). And they had a rare old time. They attacked all the cities with defences and captured every one of them. Then Sennacherib thought about going to Jerusalem to see if he could do a spot more damage. The king of Judah, Hezekiah, sent some of his servants out to meet Sennacherib's messengers. After saying hello and talking about the weather and if they'd seen any good films lately, Sennacherib's lot got down to business. They said,

"Our boss Sennacherib says—"

"Sennacherib? What sort of name is that? It sounds like a type of sweetener."

"Quiet, you fool! Sennacherib says you haven't got a hope. Give up now. The countries you thought were going to help you, won't. As for your God – he won't help you either. My Assyrian gods are much stronger than him. They've helped me conquer everywhere in the world – except England, because we don't know where it is. Don't think you can get away with it. But as I'm a generous sort of king (when I'm not killing and cutting and maiming my enemies), I'll do a deal with you then everyone will be happy. Besides which, your God himself has told me to come and destroy you all."

But God hadn't said anything of the sort. Sennacherib was just using God's name to make Hezekiah frightened. It was a load of rubbish. In fact God was angry with Sennacherib for speaking in this way.

So what do you think happened to Sennacherib? Did he:

(a) **Go back home to be killed by his sons, (who obviously didn't know about respecting their parents – look at the chapter called 'Respect your parents' to find out more).**

(b) **Go and try and discover England.**

(c) **Build a factory to manufacture sweeteners.**

(d) **Stay and destroy Hezekiah and the city of Jerusalem.**

Sins mean things that we do wrong.

If you haven't learnt that it's always the most gruesome possibility by now, then you haven't been paying attention, have you? Of course, it's (a).

Who does he think he is?

Can you think of anyone else in the Bible who got in trouble for speaking blasphemy? It's sort of a trick question because he wasn't guilty at all. It's just that lots of people said he was.

It was Jesus. On loads of occasions, the religious people of the day said he was saying stuff against God. They didn't like Jesus because he:

• Said he could forgive sins*
• Said that he was God
• Said that he was God's special person who was going to help his people
• Said he was going to sit right next to God in heaven
• Said he was going to come back to earth riding on the clouds of heaven (Sounds a cool way to travel!)

Their understanding was that anyone who said such outrageous

things deserved to be punished. And they were right. There was only one exception. It was OK to say all of these things if they were true. That's why Jesus said them.

So they were wrong. What's more, by accusing Jesus of blasphemy they were in fact doing it themselves, because they were speaking against God and his special messenger.

Do you think Jesus was telling the truth? Was he really God? And if he was/is, what difference do you think it makes to how you think?

Blaspheme? Me?
Acts 7

Paul was the most famous missionary* in the early days of the church. His hobbies included speaking to crowds, travelling, getting shipwrecked, getting beaten up, writing letters and most of all, telling people about Jesus. He did a lot of the last two, and we can read some of the letters he wrote to his friends. In one letter, Paul told his great friend Timothy that he had once been a blasphemer. This must have shocked Timothy a lot, in which case Paul may have had to write again, explaining what he meant...

Dear Tim,

Thanks for your letter. Glad the family is well and the dog is fine - wish you hadn't called him Saul of Tarsus though. What's wrong with the usual names like Rover, Spot or Habakkuk? I suppose I'd better explain why I'd written to you saying I was a blasphemer.

It happened a long time ago and I wish it never had. Back in Jerusalem there was a man called Stephen who followed Jesus. He was arrested by a group of people for talking about Jesus. They said he'd been speaking against Moses and against God. His enemies bundled him to court where he had to defend himself against their lies. But nobody wanted to listen to him. All they wanted was to see him dead. Sure enough they got what they wanted. He was stoned to death. In fact he became the first person ever to die just for being a follower of Jesus.

But the worst part of it is yet to come. I was there. I was one of those who was glad to see him die. I was delighted, because I thought I was doing God a favour. But I wasn't. I was trying to fight God. I was speaking and acting against him. I was a blasphemer. I'm deeply ashamed of it now. But I know that God has forgiven me - even of such a horrible thing. That's why I travel around telling everyone God can forgive them too. If he can forgive me for something dreadful like that, then there's hope for everyone.

Yours apostolically
Paul

PS If you get that stomach-ache again, have a drop of your uncle's best red wine.

On the television, at school, in fact just about everywhere, we hear people using God's and Jesus' names as though they're swear words or just something to say when they are surprised. Don't copy this to try to look big or clever. God is far too important to be put alongside some of the bad words we all know.

DON'T FORGET THE SABBATH.

KEEP IT SPECIAL. DON'T DO ANY WORK IN IT

The Sabbath was the name given to one of the days of the week. It wasn't meant to be like the other days of the week. God's people were supposed to make it different by not doing any work and by thinking about God.

Some people thought you shouldn t walk very far on the Sabbath. They reckoned one kilometre was far enough — except they called it 2,000 cubits instead.

Question:
Can you work out what they
would have called the marathon race, which is roughly forty-two kilometres?
Answer:
If they had any sense, or couldn t do the maths, they would have still called it the marathon. If they didn t have sense, and were good at maths, they might have called it the 84,000 cubits race.

The commandment about
the Sabbath is the longest of all of God s rules. It covers four verses. Look it up in Exodus 20:8—11.

Happy hols!
Genesis 1

When God told Moses that the Israelites were not to work on the Sabbath, he reminded him what had happened when he created everything. (You can find this story in the very first book of the Bible by looking in the front!) In Genesis, God says that it took him six days to make the universe. There was nothing left to create, so he took a day off. It was going to be a day different from all the others. God made it a holy day, which is another way of saying holiday. If it was a good idea for God, then it was definitely going to be a good idea for his people. Nobody was allowed to do any work on that day.

So if they couldn't work, what were they meant to do?

The Sabbath belonged to God and he wanted the people to have a rest. He also wanted them to think about him and have a happy time remembering all the good things he had done for them. It was meant to be a bit like having a party for God once a week.
Hang on – what's the catch?
Having a party once every seven days sounds great, but the other part of the deal was that you had to work for the other six days!

Earth Sabbath
Leviticus 25

The Sabbath wasn't only meant for people and animals. The soil was supposed to get a Sabbath too. After all, growing things for six solid years is pretty tiring and so it deserves a rest every now and then. God told his people not to plant crops for one year in seven. He promised that there would still be enough food for everyone. It must have taken a lot of trust in God to be able to do that.

Mind your mannas!
Exodus 16

When God's people were wandering about in the desert he gave them special food to eat. Every day God sent them lots of birds called quail and a type of bread which they called manna. Each time there was exactly enough food. The people didn't even have to save any for the next day. On the day before the Sabbath, God sent enough food for two days. This meant the people didn't have to work looking for food. Because there was enough grub, Moses told the Israelites not to go out scrabbling to find anything else on the Sabbath. Despite this, some people went out as normal, only to find no food whatsoever. God didn't think much of this and he told Moses so! In the end the people got the idea and instead of going doing all 'manna' of things to find God's special food, they didn't bother on the Sabbath.

I WISH WE COULD HAVE A REST FROM BEING EATEN ON A SUNDAY!

This is your final warming! God told his people they weren t to light a fire in their homes on the Sabbath. Clearly it was not cool to get hot.

I woodn't do that if I were you
Numbers 15

While the Israelites were wandering around in the desert, some of them found a man collecting wood on the Sabbath. (He'd obviously branched out on his own and hadn't twigged that others might be watching.) They took him to Moses to see what he thought of it. Even Moses wasn't quite sure, so they locked the man up. Then God told Moses that the man had to pay for working on the Sabbath. The man was taken outside the camp and punished.

When is work not work? Sometimes it was tricky to know what God meant by work. Was school work, work? Homework, work? Could you go shopping? Wash your hair? Watch a game of football? (The answer to that is no, because it hadn't been invented.) Could you do the cooking? Would you want to? And if you did, would anybody eat it?

Some of the religious leaders called Rabbis, tried to work out what was work and what wasn't.

See if you can guess which of the following they said you couldn't do:

- ☐ Homework
- ☐ Blowing out candles on a birthday cake
- ☐ Cooking
- ☐ Sewing
- ☐ Tying up an irritating sister
- ☐ Cutting and digging
- ☐ Picking bones out of fish
- ☐ Opening umbrellas
- ☐ Shaving
- ☐ Polishing shoes

The answer is **ALL OF THEM.** So you'd have to have uncooked fish fingers and find another way of keeping your sister quiet.

Re-building, re-thinking
Nehemiah 13

A man called Nehemiah helped the people to think about God again after most of the Israelites had lived in a foreign land for a long time. Together with others, he went back and repaired the city of Jerusalem, which had been destroyed by an invading army. He stopped the people making wine and trying to sell food on the Sabbath. He didn't allow foreigners to bring their goods into the city on the Sabbath. He even stopped them from camping outside the city on the Sabbath. He told the priests to guard the city gates in order to keep the whole city holy, and free from the temptation of buying and selling food on that day.

What about Jesus and the Sabbath, then?

Working out what could or could not be done on the Sabbath has always been difficult. Jesus got into a lot of trouble because many religious Jews believed he was doing the wrong thing on the Sabbath. Indeed, sometimes Jesus seemed to make a point of doing certain things on the Sabbath – even though he knew it would get up people's noses.

Hypo-what?
Luke 13

Once when Jesus was teaching in a synagogue, a woman who could not straighten her back came in. She'd been all bent over for 18 years. Jesus healed her straight away. The ruler of the synagogue said Jesus should have done this on one of the other six days of the week. In reply, Jesus called him a hypocrite. A hypocrite does not make people go to sleep and then do exactly what he tells them (that's a hypnotist). Nor is it a big animal that lives in water (that's a hippopotamus). A hypocrite is someone who tells people to do one thing and then does something completely different themselves. This is roughly what Jesus told the ruler:

"You are quite happy to untie your donkey and take it to get a drink on the Sabbath, so it's only fair that I untie this woman from the illness that has kept her miserable all this time."

That's handy
Luke 6

Once Jesus went into a synagogue, which was where the Jews met to worship. There was a man who had a badly formed hand. Jesus told the man to stand up in front of everyone. Then Jesus asked the people in the synagogue whether it was best to do good things or bad things on the Sabbath. Nobody said a word. This made him very upset, because no one was prepared to say the right thing. He told the man to stretch his hand out, and when he did, it was the right shape and he could use it again.

And what do you think some of the people wanted to do?

(a)   **Give Jesus a round of applause.**

(b)   **Say, "You've got to hand it to him, he's pretty handy when it comes to hands."**

(c)   **Get Jesus to heal their friends.**

(d)   **Plan to kill him.**

If you answered (a) you get a round of boos.

If you answered (b) you lose hands down.

If you answered (c) you're not even close.

Sadly, it was (d). Time and time again Jesus' enemies got extremely cross when he did things they thought he shouldn't do on the Sabbath.

Don't do that!
John 5

Another time, Jesus helped someone who had been unable to walk for 38 years. The man got up and started to carry his portable bed away. It was the Sabbath and the Pharisees thought you shouldn't do any carrying, so both Jesus and the man who had been cured got into trouble.

Jesus said that the Sabbath was a day to be enjoyed, not endured. It wasn't meant to be so full of hard-to-follow rules that people spent all their time trying to work out what they should or shouldn't do. That would take the fun out of it. The Sabbath was meant to be a special day for thinking about God.

When is a Sabbath not a Sabbath?
Christians still have a rest day but they call it Sunday, not the Sabbath. If they can, they will go to church to meet other Christians to think about God and take a break from the sort of stuff they do the rest of the week.

RESPECT YOUR PARENTS

Yes. At last – it's here! The rule all kids grumble about and the one every parent loves. If you look in the Bible in the book of Exodus there is an extra bit, too. God told the Israelites that if they obeyed this commandment they would enjoy a long stay in the special land he was giving them. It was an extra incentive to do what God said.

The big question is, did they manage to do it? Maybe. There don't seem to be many stories in the Bible where children were bad to their parents.

But you can hardly expect me not to spend a lot of time finding a really juicy tale of how some son or daughter had a good go at their parents, can you? You're right. And I came up with one.

A hair-raising story
2 Samuel 15

The child's name was Absalom. Now you might think that being given the name Absalom is a good enough reason not to be very pleased with your parents. Right again. But this child went a bit further than that. His father was David, probably the greatest king of Israel. And by all accounts his dad loved him very much. The trouble was that Absalom had not been behaving himself. He'd killed his brother Amnon, who in turn had done something pretty horrible to his sister. (What a family! Not the sort of behaviour you might expect from a load of royals.)

Absalom was a bit of a good-looking man by all accounts. And he liked his hair! Every time he had it cut he used to weigh it. On average it weighed over 2kg. No wonder he had to visit the hairdressers. His head must have been really heavy.

After Absalom had killed his brother, their dad wasn't too pleased and their friendship was not so much frosty as positively freezing. Even so, Absalom lived in the same town, and could see that it was pretty cool being king. So he decided he would like to be the king instead of his father. He thought that he would be a better, fairer king than his dad. I mean, we all think we know better than our parents, right? I said, RIGHT? Well, Absalom did too. So he devised a cunning plan he believed would help him take his father's place. First, he made sure that when people came to see the king, he would talk to them first. He would be very friendly and they always left thinking, "That Absalom is a very nice chap. I wonder if he'd be a good king?"

He spent four years behaving like this until he became more popular than his father. Then he decided to take his dad's place and set himself up as king of the country in a different place. When King David heard about this, he was frightened. What did he do? He ran away.

Eventually, David raised an army and they went out to fight the soldiers of Absalom. He still loved his son and gave strict orders that he shouldn't be harmed, but it was no good. Absalom was killed — and it's a hair-raising story.

Remember how he liked his hair? Well, the day of the battle, Absalom was riding his mule and he got his hair tangled in some branches. The enemy saw him and a man called Joab threw three javelins at him as he was dangling from the tree.

I THINK I'LL HAVE A **SHORT BACK AND SIDES** NEXT TIME!

There, that's the sort of story that shows you children that you should respect your parents. Either that or have a regular haircut.

You mustn't think that all children in the Bible were bad like Absalom. There were some good ones. In fact there were some frighteningly good ones. One of these was called Isaac. His story is a little bit strange – and really scary too. Just be thankful it wasn't you in his shoes.

What are we sacrificing for supper, Dad?

Genesis 22

Isaac was the son of Abraham and Sarah. He had been born when everyone thought his parents were too old to have children. This made him a very special child as far as they were concerned. One day, God told Abraham to go and make a sacrifice on a distant mountain. He happened to mention that it would be good to take his son Isaac with him too. So off they set on a three-day father and son camping adventure. But on the way, Isaac began to get a little bit worried. His father had told him they were going to make a sacrifice and usually that meant taking a sheep or a goat, but they didn't have either with them. He asked his father about it, but Dad told him not to worry because God would take care of it all.

When they got to the right place they set about building the altar, but there was still no sign of an animal to kill. Isaac was just stepping back to admire their handiwork when the next thing he knew his dad was tying him up! He was going to be sacrificed! But the interesting thing is that not once does Isaac seem to complain about it. All along he seems to trust his father completely. Most people think of this story as a good example of Abraham trusting God – and of course it was. But it was also a good example of Isaac trusting his dad and doing exactly as he was told. In the end, God provided a ram to be offered as a sacrifice so Isaac wasn't hurt in any way. God hadn't really wanted Isaac to be killed and there was no way that he was going to let it happen. It must have been a very strange experience for Isaac.

So next time your parents talk of the sacrifices they have to make for you, watch out, and hope there is some lamb in the freezer.

Proverbs and parents

The book of Proverbs, in the part of the Bible called the Old Testament, is full of wise sayings. The idea was that they made you sit up and think. Quite a lot of them are about children and parents.

See which ones you like!

A sensible son brings happiness to his father, but a foolish one shows that he doesn t really care for his mother.

Who is a shameful child? It is the one who says bad things about his father and gets rid of his mother. That child is a disgrace.

You must listen to your dad because he was the one to give you your life.

Don t think badly of your mother — especially when she gets old.

The father of a child who loves and obeys God is a very happy person.

The parent of a sensible child is always pleased with his behaviour.

If you steal from your parents then you are as bad as the person who deliberately sets out to vandalise and destroy things.

I wonder what happens to you if you are naughty and don't do what your parents tell you to do? You might lose your pocket money, have to go to bed early, or miss out on a favourite treat. Count yourself lucky! How about this?

If you make fun of your father in an unkind way or if you refuse to obey your mother, your eyes will be pecked out by ravens in the valley and eaten by vultures.

Some of the punishments in Bible times were severe.

Accused: Jebediah
Crime: Attacking parents with a stick
Reason: Wouldn't let him go out to play
Witnesses: Mr and Mrs Habadiah

"People of the jury. There is no doubt that the accused, Jebediah, has been found guilty of attacking his parents with a stick. In these circumstances I recommend that the court punishes him to the full extent of the law."

But what is the full extent of the law?

(a)   **Giving him new parents.**
(b)   **Sending him to prison.**
(c)   **Making him sow a field of corn.**
(d)   **Death.**

Accused:	Rebekah
Crime:	Cursing parents and picking her nose at the tea table
Reason:	She didn't want to eat her cabbage. There was a bogey in it
Witnesses:	Mr and Mrs Zethurial

"People of the jury. You have heard how the accused, Rebekah Zethurial, did not only curse her parents – and her mother in particular – for forcing her to eat this delicious cabbage, but she did also, at the meal table, place the index finger of her left hand up her right nostril with a view to extracting a bogey. Of these two facts there can be no doubt. She must be made an example to all children who are tempted to commit such horrible deeds."

But what is their harshness and wisdom?

(a)   **Eat her own bogeys.**
(b)   **Eat ten raw cabbages.**
(c)   **Write "I love Mum and Dad" 1,000 times in the sand.**
(d)   **Death.**

If you haven't guessed it by now, you're a bit slow. Yes. That's right. Jebediah and Rebekah both got the chop. You've never had it so good!

Looking after Grandma
1 Timothy 5

Paul, a follower of Jesus, wrote a couple of letters to a young man called Timothy (we talked about him earlier, remember?). In one of them, he said that if your mother or grandmother was a widow (a woman whose husband has died) then her children and grandchildren were to look after her. This really pleases God and it is a special way of saying thank you for all those nappies changed, tantrums suffered, pocket money given, treats... well, you get the picture.

At long last!
If you thought that this parent-child thing was all one way traffic – think again. Hidden away in the depths of the Bible is a special word to parents – dads, in particular. It says they mustn't exasperate their children. I know it sounds a bad thing to do to someone, and it is! It means your dad shouldn't make you fed up by the things that he does. His number one priority is to teach you about God and help you to follow Jesus. I bet you want to know where to find this golden nugget, don't you? Try *Ephesians 6*.

DON'T MURDER ANOTHER PERSON

For a book that most people think is full of good people and wonderful things, there are a lot of murders in the Bible. And I really do mean a lot. Killing seems to have been one of the favourite activities in those days. It all started with two brothers...

Cunning Cain Assassinates Abel
Genesis 4

Cain was the first person ever to be born. His younger brother, Abel, was the second. There was no family business to go into, so Cain became a gardener and Abel was a shepherd. One day they both brought some presents to God. Cain took along something he'd grown and Abel gave God some tasty bits of meat. God liked the meat. This upset Cain a great deal. He stewed over this for a long time. (Not a meat stew, obviously. More of a vegetable stew, I should think.)

God saw Cain was getting crosser and warned him not to do anything stupid. But Cain wouldn't listen. He invited his brother into the field and killed him.

When God next talked to Cain, he asked him where his brother was. "How should I know?" was Cain's reply. But he knew. What's more, God knew that he knew. And before long, he knew that God knew that he knew.

God was very cross and punished Cain by stopping him from growing any more food. He was forced to wander throughout the earth, never being able to call anywhere home.

Eight simple steps to kill your brother
(Do not try this at home. Don't even try and ask permission from your parents. If you do they'll only say "no" anyhow.)

1) First make sure you have a brother.
   (Sisters do not count.)
2) Become jealous.
3) Get even more jealous.
4) Get even more jealouser.
5) Repeat steps 3 and 4 as often as you like.
6) Take your brother out to a field.
7) Kill him.
8) Pretend you haven't done step 7 when God asks you about it.

AS PART OF CAIN'S PUNISHMENT, GOD SENT HIM TO THE LAND OF NOD

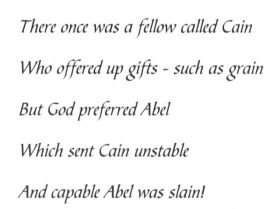

There once was a fellow called Cain

Who offered up gifts - such as grain

But God preferred Abel

Which sent Cain unstable

And capable Abel was slain!

Baby boys banished
Exodus 1

There was once a king in Egypt who was frightened of the Israelites living there. He thought they might take over the land or fight against him. So he decided on a cruel plan. He said that all the baby boys should be killed as soon as they were born. He told two of the women who helped the mums give birth, to watch whether a boy or a girl was born. If it was a boy they were supposed to kill it. But the women (whose names were Shiphrah and Puah) were faithful to God and didn't do what he said. When the king asked them what happened, they said that the mums gave birth too quickly, and by the time they arrived the child had already been born.

I don't think the king believed them because then he gave an order that every time a boy was born, it was to be thrown into the River Nile to drown. The Bible doesn't say whether many boys were killed in this way, but it does tell us that the mother of Moses* hid her son and then put him in a basket on the river, where he was later found by Pharaoh's daughter and raised as her child.

A Chilling Christmas Tale
Matthew 2

When you think of Christmas do you think of murder? Probably not. But if you look closely at the story, you'll see that there were a lot of murders. If you remember, King Herod told the wise men that he was interested in worshipping the baby Jesus. But he wasn't. The only thing he was interested in was making sure that he would be king as long as possible. So when he found out when and where Jesus had been born, he sent his soldiers in to find and kill all the boys who hadn't yet had their second birthday. An angel had warned Joseph, Jesus' earthly dad, about this and they managed to escape in the middle of the night. Others weren't so lucky. Lots of children were killed the next day – simply because Herod was a cruel man.

This was hardly the start in life a baby ought to expect. But for Jesus it was a taster of what was going to happen to him later on. If you read the story of his life you will see that there were loads of times when his enemies tried to kill him. Normally you might think that someone would try to kill another person because that person was being nasty or horrible. But people wanted to kill Jesus because:

• He healed a man's hand on the Sabbath
• He stopped people selling stuff inside the temple
• He said he would go to heaven and sit next to God
• He said he could forgive people's sins

Chuck him off the edge
Luke 4

When Jesus began telling people about God and doing amazing miracles, everybody started to talk about him. News got back to his home town. They must have been really pleased that one of their boys was becoming so famous!

So you can imagine how excited everyone was when their home-grown hero came back to town. Jesus was heading for the synagogue so the crowds squeezed and pushed their way inside, just to catch a glimpse of their very own celebrity. As soon as he opened his mouth, you could hear a pin drop. What a speaker he was! Entertaining, clever, to the point. They'd never heard anything like it. The whole town could have sat there for hours listening to him. But what they were really waiting for were the miracles. They'd heard all about them, too. Blind men could see. Sick women were cured. Children with skin rashes were made better. They knew every single one of the amazing things that he'd done. Then one person in the crowd could contain himself no longer. He was getting cramped and still there hadn't been a single miracle.

"Come on, Jesus. Show us something special. Enough of the talk. We want some action. A full-blown miracle. Show us what you're made of." There was a buzz of excitement. Yes. Yes. Yes. He's opening his mouth. He's going to do it!
"I'm not going to do any miracles here," Jesus said quietly. "You're not really interested in what I have to say. All you want is sensation and showbiz."

First of all, there was amazement. What? What's he talking about? Then attitudes changed. What right has he got to speak to us like that? "We knew him when he was knee-high to a grasshopper and now he's telling us we're not good enough for him." The noise grew louder and uglier, and uglier and louder until the curiosity turned to anger and the interest to hatred.

Soon Jesus found himself being dragged to the cliff on the edge of town, the one where he used to scramble and play when he was a boy. The raging crowd took him to the top to throw him down over the edge. But Jesus simply walked right through them as if they weren't there and went on to find some people who would be prepared to listen to what he had to say.

Missed again
1 Samuel 18

King Saul used to enjoy having David play the harp for him.

As well as playing the harp, David also wrote song lyrics. Lots of them found their way into a book called Psalms (but for some strange reason pronounced sarms). They are pretty good. We don t know what the songs sounded like, but some of the tunes have great names like **The Doe of the Morning** (not to be confused with Doe, a deer!), **The Death of the Son**, **Lilies**, and my favourite, **Do Not Destroy**.

But one time when David was playing a cool number, Saul tried to throw a spear at him. Perhaps he didn't like rock and roll? David jumped out of the way just in time and ran for his life. Saul then started chasing him all over the country to try and get him. While David was hiding in a cave, Saul came in to go to the toilet. Silently, David crept up and chopped a bit of Saul's robe off while he was otherwise engaged!

Later, David felt guilty for doing this (at least he hadn't killed Saul, which was what some of David's friends said he should have done) and when Saul went outside, he followed him and owned up. They seemed to have become friends again. But Saul was a bit of an odd character. He kept on changing his mind about some things. One of those things was whether he liked David or not. After a short while, Saul decided he didn't so he started to track David down again.

This time, while Saul was asleep one night, David crept in to his camp with his friend Abishai and they took a spear and a water jug. They then crossed over the valley to the other side of the hill. David shouted out at the top of his voice, waking Saul and his soldiers. David pointed to the pointy spear and Saul realised that he could have been killed. Once again, he decided to stop chasing after David.

You might be wondering why David never tried to kill Saul. After all, the king was making life very difficult for him. If you haven't asked yourself that question, then I will.

Why did David never try to kill Saul?

(a)   *I don't know.*
(b)   *He knew God had chosen Saul to be the king.*
(c)   *He couldn't stand the sight of blood.*
(d)   *Saul was his father-in-law.*

(a) may be true for you, but it's not good enough. The right answer is (b).

Missed again again
Acts 23

Question: Who were the hungriest people in the Bible?
Answer: Some enemies of the apostle Paul.

Why?

The apostle Paul had just been in front of the Sanhedrin – an important group of Jews. They wanted him to stop talking about Jesus. But his words made them start arguing amongst themselves. This made 40 of them very angry. They decided to silence Paul for ever by killing him. Each one of them agreed that they wouldn't eat anything again until they had managed to murder Paul. They went to the leaders of the people and told them about their plan. The idea was that they would ask the Romans (who were looking after Paul) if they could question him some more. They planned to ambush him as he was on his way. But Paul's nephew heard about it and warned the Roman soldier who was in charge of guarding Paul.

The Roman was a man of action and that very night he ordered 200 soldiers, 70 horsemen and 200 spearmen to go with Paul to another place where he would be safe. So he managed to escape from right under the noses of those bad men. They never got him, so if they were true to their word they would have died of starvation.

Missed again again again
Genesis 27

Jacob tricked his dying father into making a promise that really belonged to his brother Esau. This made Esau hopping mad. Even though Esau was the older of the two, his younger brother always got the better of him (don't even ask Esau about lentil soup!*). This was the last straw. He was going to get him this time. But their mum knew what

Check out Genesis 25:19–34 if you want to find out why!

her son was thinking (unfortunately it's something mums are often quite good at) and told Jacob to run away. He did this and didn't come back for many long years. By this time Esau was no longer cross with his brother and they became good friends again. So it does pay not to kill your brother!

MESSY MURDERS

Camping Cruelty
Judges 4

If you like camping, you may go off it after reading this!
Sisera was an enemy of the Israelites. One day, he got a load of his chariots together to go and fight. But he got beaten. Sisera decided to run for it and he went to the tent of a friend of his. The wife of his friend was called Jael (weird name for a girl!) and she invited him into the tent. She gave him something to drink and helped him lie down to rest. Soon he fell asleep. While he was snoring away, she found a tent peg and placed it on his head. Then she began hammering away.
I think I'll stick to hotels!

Chop chop
2 Samuel 4

Two guys with even weirder names than Jael, Rechab and Baanah, murdered Ish-Bosheth, one of Saul's sons, by stabbing him as he was lying on his bed. Then they cut his head off and took it to David. They thought he would be pleased. He wasn't. He ordered that their hands and feet be cut off and their bodies hung by a pool for everybody to see. That's gratitude for you.

Face it
2 Kings 8

The king of a place called Aram, was killed by a man called Hazael. He got a thick cloth, soaked it in water and put it over his face! For his trouble Hazael became the king of Aram.

In the Old Testament the punishment for murder was death. So just to make sure no one was killed when they didn t deserve it, the people had six cities where someone could run to if they had accidentally killed another person. Once there, the person could not be punished until a proper trial had taken place. If they were found guilty they would be put to death, but if they were innocent, they had to stay in that city until the chief priest died. (Quite why I don t know. So I can t even ask you to choose an answer from a list of possibilities.) Then they could go back to their home. If they went out of the city before the priest had died, a relative of the dead person was allowed to kill them!

Make friends, don't break friends
Matthew 5

Jesus said that not only it is wrong to kill someone, it's also wrong to be angry with another person. And if we call someone a spiteful name in order to hurt them, that is wrong too. He said it is much better to do everything we can to be friends with other people. When someone's cross with us, we should be the first one to try to make things right again. He said this was so important that if we were about to pray to God and realised there was something wrong between ourselves and someone else, we should stop praying and go and sort it out first.

MARRIED PEOPLE MUST BE FAITHFUL TO THEIR WIFE OR HUSBAND

Jesus said that God's plan for men and women was that if they got married, they should only have one husband or wife at a time. Most women say that one husband is more than enough, and I suppose God must have known that from the beginning. It didn't always work out like that, though, and sometimes even the greatest of God's servants had more than one wife. But if you look closely, it always seemed to cause more trouble than if they'd just stuck to one. Abraham tried it and the two women didn't get on. Jacob tried it and his wives had a competition to see who could have the most children. (For the record Leah won, but Jacob liked his other wife, Rachel, best.) King David had several wives, and it's said that King Solomon had lots of wives. How many do you think he had?

A)   30
B)   50
C)   100
D)   700

He had at least seven hundred wives who came from royal families and about another three hundred women for good measure. Just think of the birthday presents he'd have had to buy! We can only hope he was good at remembering their names.

The sad thing was that many of Solomon's wives turned him away from God. They persuaded him to follow the gods of the countries they came from. He even built idols and altars to them and made sacrifices to them. God was very cross and told Solomon that he was going to punish him. When Solomon died, his kingdom split into two and lots of the good things that he had done when he was king, were ruined.

One of God s special messengers was a man called Hosea. He married a woman called Gomer. But Gomer was not a good wife. Although they had children together she was always chasing after other men. It broke Hosea s heart to see that she didn t love only him. In his sadness, God taught Hosea a lesson. He told him that when the Israelites followed other gods or did bad things, it was like having a wife who didn t stick by you.

Run, Joseph, run!
Genesis 39

When Joseph was in Egypt, he worked for a man called Potiphar. He was a very good servant and Potiphar soon learned to trust him with everything. While Joseph was in charge, Potiphar didn't have to worry about anything at all. But Potiphar had a wife and she liked the look of Joseph. She kept trying to chat him up, but Joseph wasn't interested. He didn't want to do anything that would make God cross, or upset his master Potiphar.

One day, Joseph found himself on his own in the house with Mrs Potiphar. She tried to grab hold of him and make him go to bed with her. As she was trying this, she grabbed hold of the cloak he was wearing. Joseph managed to break free, but as he did so, he left her holding on to his cloak. Potiphar's wife was so angry with Joseph because he had refused to do what she wanted that she decided to get him into trouble. When her husband came home she lied to him saying that Joseph had been the one who had tried to get hold of her. She said she had screamed for help and she even showed her husband Joseph's cloak to prove that he had been there.

When Potiphar heard this, he turned on Joseph. He threw him into prison and left him there. Poor Joseph suffered because someone else decided they didn't feel like obeying God's rules. Many years later, the apostle Paul told Christians to run away from this sort of behaviour. I wonder if he had a picture of Joseph racing away from Potiphar's wife when he wrote those words?

OH JOSEPH! I'M **POTIPHAR** YOU!!

Jesus and the unfaithful woman
John 8

Early one morning, some of the religious leaders brought a woman who had been unfaithful to her husband, to see Jesus. They told him that Moses had said she should be killed by stoning, but they asked Jesus how he thought she should be punished. (They only did this because they wanted to try and trick him so he'd say something wrong.)

To their surprise, Jesus didn't answer straight away. Instead, he bent down and started doodling in the sand. They kept pestering him until he finally stood up and looked at them and said: "The person who has never done anything wrong should be the first one to throw a stone at her."

Then he went back to drawing in the sand. While he was doing this the oldest man there sneaked away. Then, the next oldest followed him, and so on, right down to the youngest. Eventually, only the woman was left there, standing silently on her own. Jesus got up and asked her, "Where have they all gone? Isn't there anyone who wants to punish you?"
"No," she replied.
"In that case I won't either. Off you go and stop doing bad things."

War not Phwaw
2 Samuel 11

It's spring time. The days are getting longer. The daffodils are beginning to flower. Lambs are skipping about in the fields. It's time to get ready for war. Get ready for war? What do you mean?

In the Bible times, any king worth his salt would have a battle or two once the weather was warmer. Don't ask me why, but it's probably because even tough soldiers like to stay indoors when it's cold. Anyway, all the kings were out and about, fighting here, laying siege there, ambushing in this town, massacring in that. Every king except David. He was at home in Jerusalem.

One evening, he went for a stroll on the palace roof. He caught sight of a beautiful woman having a bath. (Quite why she hadn't pulled the curtains the story never says.) David liked the look of her, so he sent someone to find out who she was.

When he heard that her name was Bathsheba he couldn't believe it! She's having a bath and she's called Bathsheba. Just imagine if she'd been having a shower – she might have been called Showersheba, which would have sounded odd, but made a good tongue-twister.

Now, because he fancied her, he asked her to come to the palace. That night they went to bed together. She went home the next morning, but a little while later she sent a message back to David. She was going to have a baby.

David knew that people would start to talk. He knew this because Bathsheba's husband, Uriah, was a soldier, and was at that very moment in battle a long way away from home. When he saw that his wife was going to have a baby, he would know that he wasn't the father. David was going to be found out. So he tried to think of a way of arranging things so that Uriah would think he was the father.

He decided to call Uriah back to the palace and pretend to ask him how the battles were going. He then told him to go back to his home to spend some time with his wife, but Uriah felt guilty at having the chance of a comfortable time, while his friends were sleeping rough in an army camp. So he didn't go home. When David found out, he tried to get Uriah drunk and send him to see Bathsheba. But even then Uriah still didn't go back to see his wife.

But the Bible says that what David had done made God very angry. Not only had he slept with someone else's wife, but he'd broken some of God's other rules too. How many had the king broken?

> • *The first one was that he longed to have Uriah's wife. He coveted her. (Coveting means wanting something that belongs to someone else.)*
>
> • *Then he slept with her. He committed adultery. (Remember, God wants married people to be faithful to their partner.)*
>
> • *Then he arranged for her husband to be killed. He ordered a murder.*

In the end, David sent him back to the battle. At the same time he secretly gave instructions to his commander, Joab. He told him to send Uriah into the frontline when they next tried to capture the town where they were fighting. That's what happened and Uriah was killed, just as David hoped he would be.

Joab sent a messenger back to David telling him what had happened. Bathsheba spent some time being sad about her husband's death. Then David invited her into his palace to be his wife.

It all started off because David looked at Bathsheba and wanted her for himself. One sin led to another. Not very nice behaviour for the man considered by lots of people to be Israel's greatest king! If you've been reading this book carefully you will, by now, understand that everybody who breaks one of God's rules gets into trouble. Despite being the most famous Israelite king, even David couldn't get out of that. So what do you think happened next?

Sheepy tale
2 Samuel 12

God sent a man called Nathan to talk to the king. Nathan told David a story about a lamb. David had once been a shepherd, so he was probably a bit of a soft touch for nice stories about sheep and animals. Besides which, maybe he liked a good bit of lamb to eat every now and again.

Nathan's story
"There was once a very rich man," said Nathan, "who had loads and loads of sheep. One day a visitor came to visit the wealthy man. 'Just hang on a minute,' the rich person said, 'and I'll get you a nice piece of tender, juicy lamb for your dinner.' But instead of using one of his own lambs, he went next door to his neighbour. His neighbour was incredibly poor and could only afford one lamb. He thought the world of it and treated it as though it was his child. Without a second thought, the rich man grabbed the lamb, took it home and served it up with cranberry sauce and roast potatoes."

David was furious. "The man should have used mint sauce and, more importantly, he should have used one of his own lambs. That man deserves to die for being so nasty."

Nathan coughed. Then he looked at the floor. Then he looked at David. "You've behaved just like that rich man. You've just condemned yourself."

David was dumbstruck. He realised that what Nathan said was true. Then he realised how wicked he had been and asked God to forgive him.

Nathan explained that David's behaviour had shown that he wasn't thinking about God and his rules at all. He had done his own thing and acted as if God didn't even exist.

What David did made a difference to the lives of lots of people. Himself. Bathsheba. Uriah. Joab. Messengers. A baby. When married people don't stick together, it always changes things for them, their children, their friends, and of course, God. One of God's ideas behind marriage was to reflect the way Jesus always loves and cares for all his followers. When husbands and wives don't stick together, it can make it hard for us to believe Jesus can stick with his disciples. But even if mums and dads are unable to stay friends, Jesus will never let us down.

DO NOT PINCH, NICK, EMBEZZLE, FILCH, PILFER, POACH, PURLOIN, SHOPLIFT, SWIPE, TAKE OR MAKE OFF WITH ANYTHING THAT BELONGS TO SOMEONE ELSE. OR TO PUT IT MORE SIMPLY:

'DON'T STEAL'.
QUITE SIMPLE REALLY.

True or false?

To help the Israelites, there were examples of what to do if someone was caught thieving. See if you can work out which of these are true.

(a) What happens if you discover a thief breaking in to your house in the daytime and you decide to take them on and have a fight and kill them? YOU GET PUNISHED!

(b) What happens if someone steals your ox or sheep and then sells or kills either of them? MAKE THEM PAY BACK FIVE CAMELS FOR THE OX AND FIVE GOATS FOR THE SHEEP!

(c) What happens if a thief can't afford to pay back what they owe you? SELL THEM OFF TO PAY FOR THE THEFT!

(d) What happens if you capture an animal thief (that is, someone who steals an animal – not an animal who goes around stealing) and the creature that had been stolen was discovered with them? GIVE THEM A RIGHT TELLING OFF, THEN LET THEM GO!

(e) What happens if you give your next-door neighbour a stolen sheep, which then gets stolen from him, and the thief is caught? MAKE THE THIEF GO TO PRISON FOR THE LENGTH OF TIME THE SHEEP HAD BEEN AT YOUR NEIGHBOUR'S HOUSE!

SHEEP STEALER

(f) What happens if you give your next-door neighbour a stolen sheep, which is then stolen from him but the thief is not caught? THE NEIGHBOUR HAS TO GO TO PRISON FOR THE LENGTH OF TIME THAT THE SHEEP HAD BEEN AT THE HOUSE!

(g) What happens if someone steals your credit card and uses it? THEY WOULD HAVE TO TREAT YOU TO A HOLIDAY AT DISNEYLAND, FLORIDA!

WOULD YOU *MIND* EXPLAINING THIS ONE TO THE CON-FUSED STOLEN SHEEP *PLEASE!*

They are all false except (c).

(a) *If a thief was killed while breaking and entering your house then you would be in the clear – except if it happened during the daytime, in which case you would be in big trouble. I wonder if that's because decent thieves in those days only went about their business at night, so anyone killed during the day can't possibly have been a crook? (!)*

(b) *The going rate for ox was five cattle and for sheep, four more sheep.*

c) *This probably meant becoming a slave and working for another person without any pay.*

(d) *If this happened then the thief would have to pay back double, double quick.*

(e) *When the thief was caught, he would have to pay back double. In this case he would have to find two sheep – as long as he didn't go and steal two more, in which case he'd have to pay back four more, and so on. (If the sheep had been staying in my house, then I'd have made them clear up the mess as well.)*

(f) *If the thief is never caught then you'd have to go to court and a judge would have to decide what to do.*

(g) *Fortunately for the Israelites, credit cards were not known at that time (and neither was Disneyland). This would probably mean that you were simply a time traveller in the wrong time zone. In this case, it would be best to forget about it and come back home.*

Sit down on it!
Genesis 31

One of the best known thieves in the Bible is actually a woman. "What did she do?" I hear you ask. (Well, this being a book I can't actually hear you – or can I?) "What did she do?" I imagine you are asking. Well, this is what she did.

A man called Jacob had been working for his father-in-law, Laban, for many a long year. Laban hadn't paid Jacob in money or gold or anything like that. Instead he'd paid him in wives! Jacob's wage was roughly one-seventh of a wife per year, so after 14 years he'd got two wives. But there are only so many wives you can have, so then Jacob began to be paid in sheep and goats.

After a while, he had so many (sheep and goats, not wives) that Laban's sons began to get jealous. They said Jacob had taken away all their father's riches. Jacob thought it best to leave, so decided to round up his wives and call his flocks, or was it call his wives and round up his flocks? Then this is what happened... oh, by the way, do you remember that Jacob's wives were called Leah and Rachel?

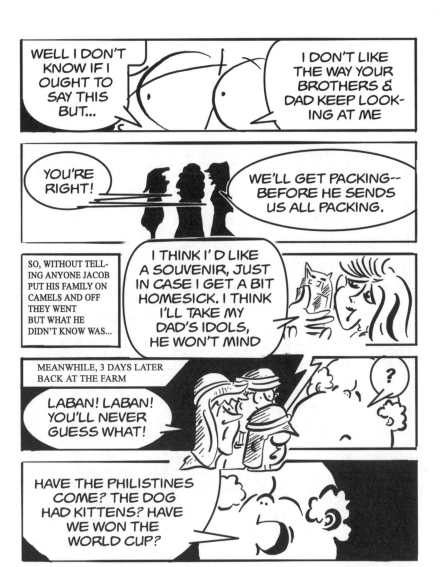

And that's how Rachel stole away with her dad's gods. And as far as we know, he never found out where they'd gone.

You might be thinking, "That's not fair. How come she got away with it?" You might not. But if you are, I'd better say something. Or two things. Firstly, not all the stories in the Bible are neat and tidy. Sometimes people do bad things and don't get into trouble, and sometimes they do good things and get into all kinds of a mess. And secondly, whilst Rachel may have tricked her dad, you and me and everyone who's ever read the story knows she was a rotten little thief. But more importantly, God knows it too. So as it was his rule she broke, she will have had to explain things to him.

Sensible sayings about stealing

Don't be proud if you've got stolen property.
Psalm 62

Everybody understands why a thief steals if he is starving hungry... but if he's caught he'll still have to pay back for what he has done.
Proverbs 6

Woe to anybody who stores up stolen goods.
Habakkuk 2

(Woe means Watch Or Else and is not to be confused with "Woah" which is usually shouted at lively horses!)

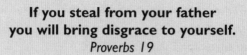

> If you steal from your father
> you will bring disgrace to yourself.
> *Proverbs 19*
>
> If a thief becomes a follower of Jesus
> they have to stop stealing and work honestly.
> *Ephesians 4*
>
> Servants shouldn't steal from their masters.
> They should be trusted in everything. If they behave like
> that their bosses will think that being a
> Christian is a good thing.
> *Titus 2*

Jesus and thieves
Matthew 6; Luke 22

Jesus told his friends not to spend all their time getting lots of money and possessions, because someday a thief could take them away. He said it was best to get things that God values because in heaven there aren't any thieves to steal them.

One of Jesus' best friends was a thief. His name was Judas. He was in charge of the money for Jesus' followers, but he kept helping himself when he wanted to. He was so interested in money that he told the people who wanted to kill Jesus where they could capture him. They gave him some silver for this information.

People steal because they think that the most important things in life are money or possessions. Jesus didn't think so. He taught his friends that other things such as love, helping people and obeying God were far more important. He also said that getting things (whether stealing them or not) wasn't as good as giving stuff away to other people. Why not try it and see if he's right?

DON'T TELL LIES

Everybody knows what a lie is. It's when we tell someone something we know isn't true. If you say you've never told one, you're probably lying!

Even some of the greatest people in the Bible told lies. The Bible tells us about them, not to make us think "if they did, then we can", but to show how easy it is for even the most respected or popular people to do the wrong thing.

Meet my... sister!
Genesis 12, Genesis 20

One of the first liars the Bible tells us about was Abraham. God promised him that his family would become a great nation. But it seems as though Abraham wasn't that sure.

He had a beautiful wife called Sarah. Once, when they were in Egypt, Abraham became worried. He was afraid that the king (known as the Pharaoh) would fancy Sarah, decide he wanted to marry her and then kill him. So Abraham told everyone Sarah was his sister. The lie back-fired. Pharaoh did fancy her, but when he took her home to be his wife everyone in his house became ill. Pharaoh smelt a rat and realised that Abraham had lied to him. The king sent everyone away (except the rat – which he killed. Well, actually that's not true. There was no rat – or if there was, we can't be sure whether it was smelly). The point is that, like most liars, Abraham got found out in the end.

The sad thing about this is that later Abraham did exactly the same thing to another king called Abimelech (I know – another weird name!). He too smelt a rat. (Sorry, better not start that again.) Abimelech liked the look of Sarah and wanted her to be his wife. As soon as she went to his home, all of his female relatives stopped being able to have children. This made him realise that something was fishy. Once again, Abraham was lying and the king wasn't very pleased. Abraham prayed for the women to be able to have babies and even though he had lied to him, Abimelech didn't seem to hold it against him.

Genesis 26
Abraham s son, Isaac,
did exactly the same thing many
years later. He lied about his wife being his sister. Surprise, surprise, it also got him into trouble!

Liar, liar!
Genesis 18

Although her husband had told her to lie on his behalf, Sarah was quite capable of lying for herself. Once, God told Abraham that he was going to have a son in a year's time. Sarah, who had been eavesdropping, burst out laughing. God heard her and asked Abraham why his wife had laughed. She said that she hadn't laughed. But God knew the truth. He simply said, "Yes, you did" and left it at that.

WHAT A HORRIBLE THING TO SAY! OF COURSE LYING DOESN'T RUN IN *OUR* FAMILY!

Genesis 3

Did you know that the first wrong thing ever recorded in the Bible was a lie? The serpent told Eve that she wouldn t die if she ate from the tree in the middle of the Garden of Eden. Later on, Jesus called Satan (because that s who the serpent was) the father of lies.

I WISH TO APPLY FOR A PATENT FOR LYING

PATENTS OFFICE

In the Old Testament, if you were caught telling a lie in order to get someone into trouble, then the rule was that you had to be punished with whatever would have been their punishment.

MISS, JEBEDIAH HASN'T DONE HIS HOME-WORK--

MAKE HIM DO THREE LOTS TONIGHT

YES I HAVE

The dog ate my homework!
Exodus 32

What's the most pathetic lie you've ever heard (or told)? Chances are that it may have something to do with explaining why someone didn't do their homework. How about this one from the Old Testament? When Moses came down the mountain after collecting the 10 rules from God, he came across the people of Israel worshipping that golden calf (the one with the earrings, remember?). When he asked his brother Aaron what had been going on, did Aaron say:

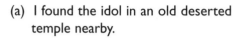

(a) I found the idol in an old deserted
temple nearby.

(b) Somebody must have brought it
with them from Egypt.

(c) Idol? What idol? You must be
seeing things. Too much mountain
air. Come and have a goblet
of wine.

(d) The people gave me their jewellery.
I threw it on the fire and the next
thing I knew there was this calf!

Well, all four explanations would have been lies, but the true lie was
(d). Aaron claimed it all happened by chance. It's a bit like saying if you
were to cut every single letter out of a newspaper, then threw it on
the floor – kapow, there's tomorrow's homework. (Don't try this. It
doesn't work - unless, of course, the homework is all about jumbled
letters.)

Be my friend?
Joshua 9

When the Israelites went into the special land that God was giving them, some of the people already living there were afraid. They decided to trick Joshua and his army so that instead of killing them, they would be their friends. They dressed up in their oldest clothes and piled rotten food on their donkeys. When they met Joshua they pretended they had come from a long way away. They asked Joshua to be their friend. He agreed, thinking they lived in a distant country. The next day he found out that they were some of the people whose country he was trying to conquer. Because he had agreed to be their friends he couldn't fight them, so they were able to live safely with the Israelites. The people were called Gibeonites, but perhaps they should have been known as the Fibeonites.

Cross my heart
Matthew 5

Sometimes, we say things like "Cross my heart", or "I promise". Grown-ups sometimes swear on their mother's grave, or on the Bible. (This doesn't mean they say rude words where their mum was buried.) The reason we say these things is to make people think that we really, really are telling the truth. But Jesus said that we should simply say "Yes" or "No". There is no need to add lots of fancy phrases to our talk. If others know that we are always truthful people, a few words from us is all they need to hear.

Did you know that in the Bible, people who lived on the island of Crete (in the Mediterranean Sea) were well known for not telling the truth? One Cretan even said they were always liars.

BUT IF HE SAYS THEY ARE ALWAYS **LIARS,** AND HE IS A CRETAN, THEN HE MUST BE LYING **TOO,** IN WHICH CASE THEY **CAN'T ALL BE LIARS,** WHICH MEANS..

Peter gets too cocky
Matthew 26

One of Jesus' best friends, Peter, was ready to die for his master. But just before Jesus was taken prisoner by his enemies, he said Peter would let him down. "Oh, no I won't," he replied. "Oh yes, you will!" Jesus insisted. "Oh, no I won't," Peter answered once more. Who was right? Here's what happened...

Pete followed Jesus to the gate
And went inside to sit and wait.
A servant girl then said, "Blow me
You're with that man from Galilee!"
Her words got Peter really narked
"Oh no I'm not," he gruffly barked.
And then another lass appeared
Who said more words that Peter feared:
"Upon my sainted auntie's breath
You're with that chap from Nazareth!"
"I'm not," said Pete - but what is worse -
He said it with a dreadful curse.
As time dragged on, some others came
And like the girls, they said the same.
"We really don't care what you say
Your accent gives the game away."
"I've told you once, I've told you twice
You nosey-parking bunch of lice,"
Peter then said, "Give it a rest!
I've never met that Jesus pest."
No sooner had those words been sowed
Immediately a cockerel crowed
And Peter - cut right to the core
Remembered words he'd heard before:
"This night before the rooster cries
You'll tell a load of porky pies
Denying that you ever knew
The friend who really cares for you!"
As ever, Jesus had been right,
Thought Peter on that tragic night.
He went outside and wept and wailed
Too well aware his friend he'd failed.

Just when Jesus could have done with a bit of support, the only person who was there with him told three lies because he was afraid he would get into trouble for being his friend.

Lying underground
Acts 5

Two of the earliest disciples* – a husband and wife called Ananias and Sapphira – sold some things. They kept some of the money for themselves and gave the rest to the church leaders, but pretended they were giving away all the money. Peter, one of the leaders, accused Ananias not simply of lying to the church, but also to God. As soon as Peter had said this, Ananias fell over and died. Later, his wife stuck to the same story (she didn't know what had happened to her husband). Peter challenged her too, and she met the same end as her husband. They both ended up lying under the ground because they'd been lying above it. Not surprisingly, all the church members were pretty spooked (and probably very honest from then onwards).

Footnote *A disciple means a follower of Jesus.

On the wrong end of lies

For every lie told, there is at least one person who is being lied to. You don't like that. I don't like it. Nobody does. Sometimes it can make a huge difference to our lives. It certainly made a difference to the life of one man in the Old Testament.

Lying about dying
Genesis 37

Joseph's brothers hated him so much they sold him to some slave traders and told their dad, Jacob, that he was dead. Even when they saw that it broke their father's heart, they still stuck to their story, preferring to keep the lie going rather than tell the truth.

Telling tales
Genesis 39

When Joseph was in Egypt, his master's wife got cross with him because she wouldn't do what she wanted him to do. She then told her husband that he had treated her badly (you remember what we read earlier about Mrs Potiphar?). Poor Joseph was then sent to jail simply because of her lies.

Most people tell lies because they don't want to get into trouble, or they want to look better than they really are. Sometimes it works but often it doesn't and they only end up in more trouble. As Sarah found out, there is one person we can never trick with a lie. That's God. He knows what we're like and what we've done. One thing you might find helpful when you think of telling a lie is to ask yourself: "God can hear me, so should I say that?"

DON'T LONG TO HAVE ANYTHING THAT BELONGS TO ANOTHER PERSON

Another way of saying this is "Don't covet". But not many people use that word anymore, so we'll stick with a simpler way of saying it.

When Moses first told the Israelites about this rule, he gave them specific examples of what they were to avoid wanting to take away from another person.
These included...

Your neighbour's house

Your neighbour's wife

2 SAMUEL CHAPTER 11

Your neighbour's male servant

Your neighbour's female servant

Your neighbour's ox

Your neighbour's ass

Anything that belonged to your neighbour; As you can see from the last illustration, you can want pretty much anything that belongs to someone else. (When I say "you can", I don't mean it's OK, I mean it's possible.) One of the obvious problems with longing to have what belongs to someone else (apart from the fact that God has told us not to do it), is that it often leads to people doing other things which hurt other people.

WOW! WHAT A FANTASTIC CARROT! I WISH I HAD A CARROT LIKE THAT!

Sul-king
I Kings 21

There is a classic example of this in the first book of Kings. As you might suspect, the book of kings is about... kings. There were good kings, bad kings, good- and bad-looking kings (try saying that with your mouth full). One of the worst of the lot was called Ahab. He was a king in some area called Samaria – get it? Oh, never mind. Ahab had a wife, but she was a bad woman. Her name was Jezebel. We join them one day at supper time...

"Ahab! Oh, Ahab, it's time to eat!"
No answer.
"Ahab! Where are you? It's your favourite. Roast beef and Yorkshire pudding!"
Still no answer.
Jezebel sets off to find him. Finally she discovers him in the bedroom. Lying on the bed, sulking (does that sound like anyone you know?).
"Ahab, darling. What are you doing up here? It's time to eat."
"Not hungry."
"Why? What's the matter? You haven't got wind again have you?"
"No. Just 'cos."
"'Cos, what?"
"Just 'cos."

"Come on dear, you can tell me. I am your wife, after all."

"Oh, all right, then. But it won't make me want to eat."

"OK, just sit there and tell me then."

"I want Naboth's vineyard."

"Oh, so you don't want to eat, you want to drink. I'll just get the servants to..."

"No, you don't understand. You know that vineyard at the bottom of the palace garden? Well it belongs to a chap called Naboth. I was talking to him today and asked him, very nicely, if I could buy his vineyard from him."

"And? I don't see the problem."

"He said 'No.' So I then offered to give him another vineyard so we could have his. It would be so convenient for picking the grapes and we could take romantic walks around it in the evening."

"And?"

"He still said 'No'."

"Pull yourself together, man. Are you a man or the king? Have one of these Yorkshire puddings and I'll make sure you get that vineyard."

"Oh, thanks. Have you got any gravy?"

After supper, Jezebel got to work. She wrote a few letters to the important people in Naboth's city.

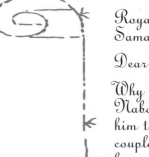

Royal Palace
Samaria

Dear Important People of Naboth's City,

Why don't you have a special meal and ask Naboth the wine grower to come along? Give him the best seat, but make sure it's next to a couple of seedy blokes. Then get them to say he has said horrible things about God and the king. Then kill him.

Lots of love and kisses

Ahab

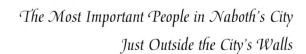

(Yes, I know Jezebel wrote it, but she made it look as though it had come from the king.)
And that's what they did. And that's what happened.
When it was all over, they wrote back, saying:

The Most Important People in Naboth's City
Just Outside the City's Walls

Dear Ahab, (or possibly Jezebel, wink, wink,
you know what I mean?)
Naboth is no longer a wine grower.
Your obedient murderers,

The Important People of Naboth's City

PS By "no longer a wine grower" we really
mean that he is dead.

Jezebel then went to speak to her husband.

"That was great Yorkshire pudding, luv. What's the secret?"
"Oh, don't worry about that now. I've got great news. Naboth is dead. You can have his vineyard and you won't even have to pay for it!"

At this point, Naboth let out a little whine of delight. And then he went to inspect his new vineyard.

And that was that. Oh, erm, apart from the dogs licking up Ahab and Jezebel's blood, of course.

What?

You see, not surprisingly, God wasn't very pleased at all with what Ahab and Jezebel had done. So he sent the prophet Elijah to go and tell them off and warn them what was going to happen to them. Missing out most of the gory details, basically they were going to be killed. Wait a minute. Why not have the gory details? It involves blood, bones, dogs, chewing and most of all, licking.

How Mr and Mrs Ahab came to a licky end
1 Kings 22; 2 Kings 9

Ahab was hit in battle by an arrow. He stayed in his chariot with the blood seeping out for most of the day. He finally died in the evening and some kind soldiers took the vehicle to a chariot wash in Samaria. They hosed it down and the blood trickled out, only to be licked up by dogs.

Later, Jezebel was chucked down from the top of the city wall. She was being chased by a man called Jehu (the one who turned Baal's temple into a toilet – remember?), who asked if someone could throw her off the wall. Some kind fellows obliged. As she hit the bottom, blood splattered all over the place. Jehu went inside and had a meal. As he was eating, he told some of his servants to go and bury her body. When they got there, all that was left were her skull, hands and feet. You've guessed it – dogs had been having their supper!

NO, I DON'T DO HANDS. TOO FIDDLY--TOO MANY BONES

F.A.C.T

Jezebel was such a nasty piece of work that her name has lived on. If a woman is particularly horrible, she may end up being called a Jezebel.

Simon says: "I want that!"
Acts 8

Simon was a magician who lived in a city in Samaria. He was very famous and a bit of a big-head. When one of Jesus' disciples, Philip, came to town, Simon became a Christian too. He was so keen he used to follow Philip everywhere. What he most liked about Philip was the great miracles and powerful signs he was able to do.
One day, two more of Jesus' disciples arrived: Peter and John. They met all the new Christians, prayed for them and put their hands on them to bless them. When they did this, God's Holy Spirit entered the new Christians, to give them special power from God.

Simon looked on, amazed. Amazed and jealous. It was about as clear a case of wanting what someone else had, as you could possibly imagine. He desperately wanted to be able to do that – just be able to dish out the Holy Spirit. That would have been better than all his magic tricks put together. He'd be even more famous and respected. So he asked Peter and John if he could buy the ability to hand out the Holy Spirit. To be perfectly honest, Peter wasn't that impressed with the request. "You can't buy this sort of gift with money. It's a special gift from God. He gives his gifts to who he wants, not the highest bidder. Your thinking is way off-line. You'd better sort yourself out and ask God to forgive you."

To his credit, Simon saw that he'd made a bit of a mistake. So he asked Peter and John if they would pray to God so that he might not be punished for his bad thoughts.

This story shows that it's not just other peoples' things that we can want. We might want their looks, skills or friends too.

When God sent his people into the special land he was giving them, he told them they were to destroy any idols they found. He also told them not to even think of melting them down and using the gold and silver. Everything had to be destroyed. But sadly, not everyone obeyed.

No takin', Achan!
Joshua 7

When the Israelites attacked the city of Jericho, everything that was of great importance had to be put in a special place. Joshua, the leader, thought that everyone had obeyed this command, but when the soldiers went out to fight the next battle, they were easily beaten. Joshua realised that something had gone very wrong.

The bad news for Achan was that he was taken outside the camp and executed because of what he did. The good news for Joshua was that the next time the Israelite soldiers fought a battle, they won.

Very often, wanting what belongs to another person can lead to us doing other bad things like stealing and thinking only of what we want. God expects his friends to think of others and what they might like to have or do, instead of just wishing we had the latest toy or game.

THE END BIT:
GOD RULZ, OK?

Ten isn't a huge number of rules. I bet your school has more rules than that. And yet as we've seen, lots of different people in the Bible found it pretty easy to break them. Sometimes, like David, they managed to break several of God's rules all in one go. Can you remember what Nathan said to him? (Look at page 85-86.) He said David hadn't been thinking about God at all. He'd just behaved how he wanted to and forgotten about God. Because David was king he thought he could do what he liked. But he couldn't. He wasn't the ruler. God was. Or better still, God is. Today.

It's not just people in the Bible who broke the 10 rules. People break them now. I do. You do. We all do. Whether it's telling a small lie, not doing what our parents tell us, or always wanting things that belong to other people.

Breaking one or even several of the rules is just the same as telling God we don't want to do things his way. That's the real problem with disobeying one of God's rules. Not only do things go wrong (show me a story where someone broke a rule and everything was OK!) but it's like turning our backs on God and saying we're not interested in him or the good plans he has got for us. It's like telling God we've found a better way to do things. But the 10 rulz were made to help us have a good and happy life.

God wants people to enjoy life and to be able to live peacefully with each other. And the only way that can happen is when everyone obeys the 10 rulz. When everyone understands that God rulz. OK?

If we're honest, we'll have to admit that we've not really cracked it. No one, not even Bible people, did everything right all the time. Except Jesus. He never broke a single commandment, and he said he would help his friends to avoid breaking them too. Jesus said the first step to becoming his friend was to understand that they don't rule.

That God rulz.

OK?

God Made Snot

Greetings!

Let me introduce myself. I'm Professor Abednego Smott, one of the world's leading snotologists and a specialist in the sciences of Body Gunk and Sticky Green Stuff.

In *God Made Snot!* I will be investigating the Five Crucial Questions of Advanced Snotology:

Number 1: Who made snot? and Number 1-and-a-half: Was it God?
Number 2: If God made snot, why did he do it?
Number 3: What is it for?
Number 4: What might looking at snot tell us about other things God made?
And Number 5: Is it time for tea yet and are we having bubble and squeak (although mainly I'll be asking that as a private thought in my own head).

Right then. Give your nose a blow, unwrap the tissue and have a good look at it for a while (gorgeous!), throw it away somewhere safe, grab a copy of this book and read on...

£4.99 (price subject to change)

Available from your local Christian bookshop or (UK orders) from: Scripture Union, PO Box 5148, Milton Keynes MLO, MK2 2YX. Or call Mail Order direct on 08450 706 006. Also available online at: www.scripture-union.org.uk/publishing.

Please add £3.00 p&p for mail order (UK).